Praise for

my husband holds my hand because i may drift away & be lost forever in the vortex of a crowded store

In *my husband holds my hand because i may drift away & be lost forever in a vortex of a crowded store,* john compton crafts a poignant narrative of tumultuous corridors and the profound experiences nestled within and beyond. Through evocative prose, compton explores themes of identity, survival, and the quest for connection amidst the chaos. In the author's own words, "dark corners & small back tables" serve as sanctuaries. From the haunting specter of violence to the transformative power of love, each passage resonates with raw emotion and profound insight on the tender beauty found in human connection. *my husband holds my hand because i may drift away & be lost forever in a vortex of a crowded store* is a captivating exploration of life's delicate balance between darkness and light.

—**Angelique Zobitz**, author of *Seraphim*

A careful balance of hardship, overcoming, and instructions for living in a society that condemns your very existence, john compton's *my husband holds my hand because i may drift away & be lost forever in the vortex of a crowded store* is a roadmap for the poet's poetic and personal life. This collection centers the body and elucidates its vulnerabilities. Imagery moves quickly from frightening to touching. compton displays a deft hand at taking the grim and finding beauty.

—**Mark Danowsky**, EIC of *One Art: a journal of poetry*

The title of john compton's collection, *my husband holds my hand because i may drift away & be lost forever in the vortex of a crowded store*, epitomizes the poems within: they own a contemplative intimacy with the quotidian. Some strike as a Zen koan, like "eleven things i like about summer" final stanza: "i like it as much as when you said / that making love was like / making love to nothing." It is a moment—like many points throughout the book—of intellectual elusiveness *and* emotional familiarity that begs to be meditated upon. compton's use of ordinary things in his images particularly makes his sex poems delightful and devastating. In "all i could do was swallow," he declares: "i cum like breathing a bridge / to help you cross," and at the end of "fetish mantras," he observes: "face down: *the cotton / is egyptian—the thread count, expensive.*" While the lyrical "I" in "our stream of consciousness" may believe his "kiss / doesn't perpetuate homosexuality," I happily report that compton's poems do! And I'm here for this queer agenda!

—**Daniel Lee**, author of *Anatomy Of Want*

my husband holds my hand because i may drift away & be lost forever in the vortex of a crowded store, by john compton is, among other things, a clear-eyed examination of the body, its hungers, desires, shames, and pains. It's a book of desires fulfilled, thwarted, and manipulated. The poems explore "my body," "his body," "your body," and "her stone body." Bodies that are "mercy," "burning," "rakish," and "dampened." They are manuscripts in which life is engraved, or poems spilled out of autopsy with stories that "carved poetry into my back." There are "dirty boys" and "sadistic cum stains." For compton, sex is both burden and gift, its fluids and actions work like spells that transform the speakers' wounds into incantations of survival. A "new body . . . instead of stretch marks, / . . . has a multitude of hieroglyphics / scratched across its walls." In love with the language his body has held and both born and borne, compton's poems resonate with a deep pulse of the indomitable life force of a survivor: "the naked body   a rosary / bead tucked in each wound."

—**Subhaga Crystal Bacon**, author of *Transitory*,
shortlisted for the Lambda Literary Award

john compton's collection of new and selected poems *my husband holds my hand because i may drift away & be lost forever in the vortex of a crowded store* is an arresting display of surprising lyricism and visual music, hymns of desire and longing that unfold like a song buried inside since boyhood. "the simplest things are erotic. i'm trying to learn love, but no one will teach me. . . i sat too close to crying too close to throwing my body off the edge too sentimental too gay." At times voyeuristic, these poems have an accepted sadness folded into them, a wandering of imagination, a surrealist tone that evokes another world of escape. "we're at the end & fraying: collect me in your fingers . . . we wander into a foliage folding into a thousand honeybees. his face, two sets of flowers: those planted, & those wild." There is hard-earned beauty here, within these lines, within these pages.

—**Kai Coggin**, author of *Mother of Other Kingdoms*
and *Mining for Stardust*

john compton's *my husband holds my hand because i may drift away & be lost forever in the vortex of a crowded store* is a wonderful permutation of pain, paradise and pleasure. They write, "i engrave poems/into flesh on his back,//clean the wounds with alcohol/ so scars heal legibly." This feral collection is continually like that.

Imagistic, bewildering, surprise surprise surprise. A book of fractals fused by love, both jagged and bewitching.

—**Luke Johnson**, 2024 California Book Award Finalist, author of *Quiver* (Texas Review Press) and *Distributary*

my husband holds my hand because i may drift away & be lost forever in the vortex of a crowded store

FLOWERSONG
PRESS

poetry by

john compton

FLOWERSONG
PRESS

FlowerSong Press
Copyright © 2024 by John Compton
ISBN: 978-1-963245-74-5

Published by FlowerSong Press
in the United States of America.
www.flowersongpress.com

Cover Art by Tavo Arrieta
Set in Adobe Garamond Pro

NOTICE: SCHOOLS AND BUSINESSES
FlowerSong Press offers copies of this book at quantity discount with
bulk purchase for educational, business, or sales promotional use. For
information, please email the Publisher at info@flowersongpress.com.

table of contents

new poems

a child growing wild inside the mothering womb

ampersand

my husband holds my hand
because i may drift away &
be lost forever in the vortex
of a crowded store

new poems

high school

was a zoo.

dark corners
& small back tables
were my nesting ground.

i found devotion
in the margins of my notebooks,

learning each poem
like a new sibling.

i studied their hands & faces
because eventually
they would die—

their bodies:
firebrand.

high school was also

a hunting ground;
poachers with their rifles.
they never killed, but maimed:
the enjoyment was tracking their prey.

one day

three students threatened
to tie me to a bumper
with rope & drag me

until i was roadkill.

i could only imagine
how long it would have taken;
my blood slick like oil.
the pavement having held an honor.

it was dark.
their threat muddied
by a man
talking on the television.

(third person)

we're at
the end
& fraying:

collect
me in your
fingers—

slide me
through
the eye

to mend
us

or release
me
so that
i do not
dangle

gravid

you tore
me
            open
like an orange

in
half, &

peeled back
                my skin
to
emerge

tender community of fabled people

i stammer out of a growing perplexity.
i ask an awkward boy to show me how
i'd lost myself,
who moves lightly over grass.

i continue the passage of identity:
something is asunder in its laughable zone.
we wander into a foliage
folding into a thousand honeybees.
it's a modifier of time
to obtain memories by swindle.

he is a child's head, the man whom i found, who leads me,
speaking about the lack of history & exaggeration:
the world is heavy with down—
vision & terror
for those who make earth black & white.

he is a match burnt-out. drunk once
from personnel,
now sobering
from them. i tell
the child-head he is as queer as i.
his eyes swim with curiosity.
his face, two sets of flowers:
those planted, & those wild.

i watch him grab a tree & shake it.
leaves rattle like tambourines.
out farther from that music:
a religion of birds chirp like a strange sea.

halfway to somewhere, there was
a green floral of ferns.
a casual display of tiny waviness.
the child-head spins around
with an odd illustration. i've never seen
a man swoon.
he drifts backwards, his arms like wings,
& the ferns took him into their leaves
like a pool's vile waters.

nothing is without error. i stand there
& hesitate to smile;
but he clamors his way back to his feet
& says, *your anxiety might*
have suggested my death.

we tread into a pine forest.
needles sow the ground.
i had needles once, sewing butterflies
& beetles inside
picture frames.
there is a dignity in everything.
i licked their wounds with thread.
my fingers lumpish, their bodies
segmented & hollow.
i was a giant out of place.

the sun breaks through,
digging its way to our faces.
the child-head strolls with certainty
through the twisted maze.
i lag along. this was an honest walk:
i am a gnome out of place.

we make it to a community of buildings.
at a glance, the windows are mirrors
& reflect everyone sent out to work.
the bus stop whittles me down.
i turn my face to his.
i notice his eyes: their milky gaze.

poem for the poets like me

for William "Bill" Corbett

"I want only the mystery of your arms around me.
Dont worry about eating my food."

— John Wieners, *"Sickness"*

i lie on my ragged loveseat
    fluff pulled from broken seams
    cotton to catch
the poems i read by john wieners

loving the men he was around
    envious
ones i will never meet

ones i'll only drink up with words

    & the blue morning provokes
the wind which pushes hundreds
of brown leaves to the ground

    i feel their wings on my skin
the skin that yearns for touch

    but the hands that own me are only photographs
& i'll have to wait to know
whether i'm still a reason to declare war

i reach out to this lonely room
    with a computer & chair
& the radio screaming songs
from sundry artists

    to write my hallelujah poems

to scatter them across the body of men
    across the bark of trees
across the hills i walk over to get me

    to a garden full of mouths

the war beside the street

when we were children
my sister, uncle, & i
played war:

there were no dangers
in any large rock
we hurled—

the dumpster,
tree, & abandoned car
made great shields.

we'd peek around,
narrowly missing,
our skulls barely not cracking open,

then laugh
when the other missed.
luckily, we'd always miss

as they'd smash
into anything
they came in contact with,

ricochet & roll.

we never had prisoners
of war, just white flags.

dinner became
our mutual
enemy,

the kitchen
transformed
into a demilitarized zone.

the seeds

the moth sits
on a tea leaf—
river fog rises

—

a minnow gleams
from murky water—
fisherman bait

—

light diffuses
through glass—
ghosts

—

the coffee pot
drips hymns—
awakened

—

a flowerpot
tends the seed—
mother & child

seclusion, or

why embrace
    in the way touch would be
a private moment, completed:
    an electrical charge,
making light. sweat shocks us.

hide things
    in your mouth—the sacred—
tug at knowing.
    forget
our language, *to*
grasp an instant but nothing beyond
feelings—one night

    or day, if the curtains are closed.

artwork, or possibly birth

you detach her right ribcage
& then her left—

they open like wings.

on earth we're briefly gorgeous

we came to share the same body
full of chemotherapy—

the healing poison flows through us
after he's finished, after he gave me part
of himself.

he lay there, tired & estranged—
his thoughts are in the process of connecting

each tissue, each muscle to roll his body,
so i can embrace vulnerability.

look into the river at all the small poems

typewriters congregate
in the river. water
flows through the keys.

papers swim through
ribbons, their fins
collect ink, collect solitude,

absorb words, address the ends.
the black begins to convolute.
their thin bodies swim

into the lake
full of paperbacks & the shoal
gathers into a book.

the cause of the apocalypse

this violin lying in the corner,
wearing dust like a cape,
played bach's chaconne so violently
the trees
danced
until they exploded into a war of splinters
& everything stopped.

lifeline

i wear your cancer
around my neck
like a pendulum

your swaying
of time
rests on my chest

so far
the rhythm
keeps up
with my
heart

& your life
sits comfortably
waiting for the wasps
to crawl
from their larvae

i mowed your facial hair,

aligned the edges
of your cheekbones;

i filled mulch
inside your mouth

planting my garden.

we lie awake;

the stars
are blond eyes
watching us;

& the first seed buds,

& as a family
we memorize its first leaf,
its first petal, its first bloom

& we name her lily.

i tattoo *miss you sleeping*

across each eyelid.

fingering tiny sweat beads
to the side, they sit there
& touch your body
like the little whores

you fuck with.

please realize: you'll understand
my absence loves you
when i attach sex to your lips
like burnt matches.

i play with the hatter, mad

we drink tea, play sane,

    & spoon.

i was opened like an autopsy

for my stories

to be shared.

these secrets

that should be held

within a fence.

eight & a half years

of solitary

carved poetry into my back.

though scars have healed,

the effect

sealed its fate.

my body, my bones,

my blood:

i am heredity.

our stream of consciousness

gets us naked. they pick names
for each part of our anatomy.

bare to the open space
their devotion
is to catch us, call it
prostitution, & pay us
with condemnation.

their eyes study our bodies
making us hard as statues
in this war zone.

they think we're imperfections:
my kiss
doesn't perpetuate homosexuality;

your sex is a touch
of love.

i study the outtake of your masturbation

wet lines—
like rows of maggots
in transition.

you whispered beautiful things
summoning them from hiding.

i take air from my nostrils

& blood from my veins

to place it inside
the life no one believes
exists

because you don't yet look human
so they disqualify you
as my child

we've built lies

out of scrap metal.

now we sit
broken & silently
pulling

rusty nails.

he came into my room for a reading

i engrave poems
into flesh on his back,

clean the wounds with alcohol
so scars heal legibly.

i make his body
my manuscript,

publish him
in my bedroom.

i pretended that he liked me

his smile created a fissure.
thoughts streamlined.

i needed intimacy,
but his lips never moved—

i contemplated being alive;
the fulfillment i caused in another.
we spoke but he didn't understand.

i could never be naked in his sight;
yet all i wanted was to be naked,
bared in the most beautiful way.

when he stretched
i read the elastic band on his underwear,
a brand i didn't know.

the simplest things are erotic.
i'm trying to learn love,
but no one will teach me.

i curled up in bed with the cold.
it touched my cheek,
leaving marks
like bruises i couldn't hide.

to a young poet

let your poems be fingertips
that maneuver from their eyes
to their mouth
& sit on their lips.
make them recite poetry
they could never fathom.

i birth

your blue
nightlights touch me, not
with softness
but precision. they cut
that edge of fear
so i sleep
not with nightmares but
with bones that form your body,
muscles that i can feel tighten
& blood
which smears us
conjoined.

a conversation

i've got shoes inside my head.

shoes?

yeah, you know—
they say i'm crazy.

oh! you mean *issues.*

no! not *his shoes,*
my shoes.

we wear them.

eleven things i like about summer

when it's dark,

raining,

or colder than usual.

when i'm in the air conditioning.

when i pretend it's the apocalypse

& the sun has exploded.

i like summer when it's not in season.

i like it better when i lie

about how much i like it.

when it doesn't

glue my clothes

to my skin.

i like summer like a nightmare

i can't wake from,

the one where i run too slow

& the monster always eats me.

i like summer like how leukemia

destroys the body.

i like it as much as when you said

that making love was like

making love to nothing.

as i become a man

the cave draws in coolness.
my lungs opened—
air exploring the dwelling.

the wet walls prompted thoughts of mother,
how she held me close
inside her womb & sang lullabies
as though she heard me cry.

i pushed & rebelled,
one day escaping but returning.
i sought refuge in arms
that i knew, but were new.

the outside came to me
with its knowledge
& my mother touched my lips
to silence & listen.

the cave is my mother.
it quiets me & i hear
the lullaby's that echo
off her walls.

the boys in ordinary clothing

i have made lovers with poems.
people tell me it is unhealthy
yet they never replace the poetry.

i sit in rooms full of white
& lie down.
i've lied on sheets of paper:
new, crumpled, torn.

how warm is the poem?
his eyes full of ink.
his skin sweating lavender.
his moans heave emotions.
his tongue writes
use me, use me, use me.

the box of graves

you're autumn
though green eyes
suggest spring.

but in breaking,
each dead thing departs
easily.

left with the heart,
a toy misplaced
inside a chest,

plastic & dumb,
it plays like a child's harmonica:
all sound, no melody.

your body plants itself
with pink muhly grass

because you want to spread
like wildflowers

but know you aren't as beautiful.

you fought stars
falling
too quickly
to give light—

finding darkness,
spiders roll your hair
into small balls—

making silky pearls
& using them as egg sacks.

papercut society

poetry is cut
from my stomach;

removal of self
in written words;

inside the mess
of blood.

i pledge allegiance
to our two-faced flag

& pay taxes
so that my rights may be taken.

lower-class means
not really a citizen—

i should build a wall
to keep out the government;

but they'll just feel excited
by the prospect of war.

i love you means:
the water heater has broken

again & you're the only one
who can fix it;

while *president* means:
fuck you, you're too poor.

i am a believer of
"oh god"
but not
"dear god"
or "please god"
but occasionally
i'll believe in
"god help me"—
with sarcasm.

i'm practicing to be a pornstar

i've seen gorgeous men
aligned in rows
with horoscope eyes
pledging a truth

who beg for my mouth,
all at once, but louder—
& then pray for repentance.
they know i'm built for intake.

i let them pass my lips:
jets, landing fast on my tongue
to acquire me—if they taste
as they've made themselves appear.

their cocks are anvils
that weigh me down—
the lust of their semen
are slurs pouring out.

surrealism & manipulation of the eye

you are a rebellious lithographic lover
with frayed edges that tear
at the slightest touch & your blackest
ink fades into my skin.
  the residue announces:
our bed is made of wishbones;
we steal the rings of saturn
to wear them as holy things;
our darkest corners are alive.

all i could do was swallow

when i cum in a dream
    no one
asserts my man-made creation.

it's not because you're there,
or not, or somewhere whispering
sexual assaults but

i cum like breathing a bridge
to help you cross:
the orgasm quaking the joints
in my body—

      when i cum
it becomes an exhibit.

i lay your head on my chest
& aim at your mouth.

sex fiend

the fox captures
my perversions in his teeth,
jaw clamped like a virgin.

i use my dick & usually
they taste something
other than death,
even after swallowing.

i wear maggots under my tongue
& keep a shoebox filled with tic tacs:
if anyone asks, i show them a little white mint
but blow maggots up their ass.

i felt like a song
on a record
in a jukebox:
the scratching leads to pleasure.

fetish mantras

a head full of the spider's web
floats through sex
with a poisonous bite—

inept & frivolous,
they spin lies & contempt
toward the body.

i lay in bed,
a crescent moon,

& his hand is an asteroid
slamming into my ass:

the hot layer cools in the dark.
suffocating, the want

to drink his breath is primal.
his cock is a telescope.

i examine
the depth of him.

are we done here?
the matchbox asks.

burning his pubic mound
& licking the wild ashes
off sheets.

face down: *the cotton*
is egyptian—the thread count,
expensive.

masochists

sometimes i pretend
i am a paper airplane
when the boys touch me—
i fold
at all my ligaments
sharp & crisp
& wing myself free,

though i land back in bed
with remnants of dirtier boys;
with sadistic cum stains
outlining bodies.

ode to my first sex toy

when i was young
i had sex with the couch—
between cushions.

my kid cock
pumped the tight
in-between of fabric
until the tickling
of cum

darkened the stitching.
the thick liquid
making its mark:

i was his lover.
he belonged to me.

i was never taught masturbation.
never realized
what caused the hardening
or pleasure—

the secret i learned,
the hushed thing i did,
i knew i was the *only one*
that would do such a grotesque thing.

learning to love my new body

a wet temple: exploration
goes almost mute,
decades pass before someone realizes:
        thick form

is beauty—is real—is natural.
is not bone but coral. is not
the puddle drying daily in the sun
but ocean

hungry & fierce
& organic.

instead of stretch marks,
my body has a multitude of hieroglyphics

scratched across its walls.

my dirty language

rummages your mouth:
the too-clean teeth
are perfect canvases.
i paint vintage nudes,
turn your virgin tongue
into a palette.

your thin bottom lip
makes an exceptional
brace. i use it
to prop my wrist.
it calms the tremors:
the diaphragm of my mental health.

i like how your saliva
cuts through the paint.
it makes a mess of your body.

we didn't start here, but moved
intricately to you wanting to live
a different life.

you were tattered by the end
& left surrendered. the light
pouring out—& gradually you knew;
you tasted the taint.

a child growing wild inside the mothering womb

ghost city press, 2020

the little abilities of night walking

i search through my boundaries:
beyond cracks of light,
moon-halos & silhouettes.

the chair sits strangely
in the corner. his arm grazes
my leg & the door
creaks: a ghost open.
everything is whispery
in the lonely.

the little bones underfoot
crackle seamlessly.
i step across her hardwood stomach
& it groans, each one
less likely visible.

cool air brushes goosebumps
along my arm skin. my hairs rise
like snakes.
    trees are mindless
in sleeping
dreaming in their leaves
rattling nightmares play
games in my mind.

the moon is a small red slit which looks like the bottom lip of a bitten smile

the moon bit his bottom lip
& blood rose under-skin.
the red slice wavering
his graywater mouth.

he knew fragmenting clouds—
dissolved—
left you stranded in some memory-
dream he could barely remember.

his excitement for thunderstorms
became manic. he gritted his teeth,
trying to fraud thunder
& convince the sky to rain.

winter poem

mouth open
letting snow cover my burial plot
of words

& fingers too cold to dig
the tongue out:
frozen corpse,

the stature of teeth chirping
a ruptured hymn

poem from a cell phone with minor edits

the trees
were going through their impotence
& we had to wait for a while
between sheets of paper

*

& i could see
her mother was like her mother—
when she said something about the bed,
she spoke her child back to sleep

*

our busy day of treatment finished
with the other person who had cancer
& what you want
is to be uncleansed by the same results
like a curtsey or a cold shower

the color of wasp bodies cover my blanketed mind

the stinger erupts as sound
hurtled behind my eyes

because sometimes my poems
collapse at the end

veins burst   blood
rushes into the dams of my pupils

their structure falls apart
      broken rafts, faux hopes

& wings of wasps, paper-
thin but metallic in light
   are the same lies my verse
will feed you—edible
for only a time until you realize

not all things were birthed
from wombs, but some
delivered by maggots

presentation of an old discovered species

you wanted a harbor safely
harnessing you to the beach
   the salt-air to sift through
your mouth like taffy—rejoicing
in the sand: exfoliating
your dampened body

anchoring to a known
sunday with a song laden
with some holy scripture
that you can recite
to focus the pain into a hymn
sending it to god

the stillness comes & you
pretend the pounding
of bombs between your thighs
are waves / his eyes
become lighthouses beaming
ships away—too far to comprehend

you are as pretty as before;
he ripped away your words
& forced them underneath
his shoe like roaches—
his hand smelling like bleach
trying to wash away your voice

doors, doors, doors

i remembered when

i was remembering
how the moon

isn't hollow
the craters aren't entrances

it is but it isn't
a mimic of the sun

though the wholeness
pushes the ocean
onto the beach

like blankets
we both crawled

opposite

revealed the coldness
we kept

suffocated in the appearance
of happiness

we
create a hurricane too vicious

& close the highway
so there is no clear path

i read signs
like scripture

light comes out our mouth
each time we scream

illuminating fish bones
that we've expelled
& collected around our room
like barriers aloft

we seeded him holy

you'll find him in a chair
sequenced

   gay   is   vandalism

we used white rags &
    smoke   to purify him

to bleach the sin, to poach the black resin
from the heart-skin
to bring him
               right
by rules of man

his arms & ankles tied
    crosswise
the naked body   a rosary
       bead tucked in each wound

dreamers of a real world

i keep looking back
at my hands
those neatly-folded
little wings   though i could not fly
could not escape the pain
of boys   their games   their
sticks & stones & words
their masculinity, which engraved
their whole bodies

i sat   too close to crying
too close to throwing my body
off the edge   too sentimental
    too gay

holy scripture man

your chest becomes
my confessional. i touch the flesh bible
daily & let sins
flood my fingertips
into your heart   my repentance

your voice is a soothing hymn.
    your tongue a sharp blade.

i mostly feel like destroying prayers
    screaming the words
until the pain loosens & knowing
only god   is you

only you   are there
    to receive me

fuck donald trump

morning waits
    lying in the weeds

a sniper aimed & patient

to impeach freedom
from thought

to pardon itself:
anti-war criminal

your war hand holds grenades
not peace   not softness
but explosions

notice what you've done
    disguising what love is   love
has done   has come from
what love is love anymore

i touch my forehead
as a decree
    you saturate yourself
    in a smokescreen

ampersand

plan b press, 2018

the house in the attic

pretending is flying with new stability

i drop
ink
onto paper
like
machine gun
shells

the city is burning
all her people to the ground

i am focused
said the blind man
with his eyes rattling in his pocket

the door that once opened
there is nothing of that home
anymore

—

a ripple under my skin
    fish
rising
to feed on ants
caught in the wake

i try to open the sky

getting behind clouds
i pry, peeling them toward the ground
with a crowbar

as snow gets here
it whitens my mind
then rebels

cleans the gutters of my brain

thank god for the numb

though pain is a monster
& they'll wait
at the brim

until it fades a hair thin

eventually
to be perforated

rendering nothing
but screams

———

the envoy of worry
collides with the soundless regime

pitchforks reside
in the violent testimonies

coming in dreams
her stone body turns fleshy

she has a need to whisper
her nightmares

to excavate the pebbles
from her head
knocking in her skull

her feet remain sanctioned
to the base

never free

she pushes past the hardening
to free the last words breaking her lips
her eyes dull
my sight fragments

she is gone

—

do you want to go
through flowers

lay in the bed of petals

let my head, a bulb
be planted   rooting
inside your chest

& you'll transfer your renegade hands around me

& you'll take the wet clay
remolding us
into what we should have become

because we were too busy forgetting
& changing into things
we thought we were meant to change into
carefully becoming each other's mirage

look into the portrait
of your eye
the shine produces
exact replicas

—

their whistles are wind
sliced by whips

derogatory sounds
that make me shudder

blowing my clothes off
with their mouths

naked, bent over, penetrated
already in their heads

carnivores
chasing prey

taking me down
we roll

a thick dust cloud
chokes us

we lie there in sweat
& grout

we lie there breathless
& sound

i won't be bound
i stand up

& take myself
somewhere else

summer months
burn & fade

we tie the dying
over flames

to cleanse their souls
before they are taken

to the paradise
that waits

—

there is something
magnetizing:

when departed
you're easily   forgotten

here   in skin
an obsession

i can't figure out

you hold the voice to my ear

i turn into something that you eat
& crawl behind your teeth

engrave love words or letters
or statements in the enamel

to be read & reread

but you remove your jaw

my reentry from your mouth
into the noise

has me lost & humiliated

crayons melt
why in the hell can't you love me
we are like children
spontaneous & learning

i find each individual freckle
& memorize it

you are the game i take for granted
never finishing

—

a boy
too smart for his age
he loves
how to learn

he breeds his words
disposing runts
producing the strongest verse
& sees in his manuscript
best in show

you belong to your birth
the long nights of conception
the way you came with your flood
you reach from her second mouth
rip open the lips & force yourself out

you demand
dictator
to be seen
heard
hailed

—

symptoms exist
in the precipitation

the sky
over-exaggerates
the cause of illness

the thunder of his stomach
rumbles across wearily

clouds disperse
as he sweats out his fever

the blue reemerges

—

i breach
into small occasions

little lifeless insects
collect to rid themselves
of soul
passing around the poisoned pellet

for absolution

the ants build their bodies
into monuments

so that the next generation
can study such sacrifices
in order to understand
their survival   their loss

—

my fingers absorb into the keyboard
infusing knowledge into their nominal actuality

the green tube
contains the deaf sound

you'll never squander
the listening

—

i draw windows
& stab my pen through the glass
to uncramp

what's inside my head

force me
inside-out
& scrape the meat from the peeling

leaving a field-dressed carcass
dry my hide
& sell it as an exotic leather

my father's wars
were different

his were fought with guns & stealth
i fight mine with pills

& liquor

i drink until
my mind becomes a shield

deflecting everything

& memories

i put your mouth on mute

we become stone walls

chisel us
until we can breathe again

before we become fossils

—

the moon
is noon's
pimple

blemishing
the sky

chase away the demons
that escape from the unlocked box
inside my skull

that the doctor had left open
because inside there held
a masterwork

he tried to plagiarize

did you find the key

to my sanity?

—

i regress
into nothing but sleep

to which my brain
becomes obsolete

& someone says
"i've seen your brother"
who doesn't exist

or does he?
my dreams are unfocused

i wake to an unstable environment

something like heaven

—

my brain is as godly
as the angel who touched
my heart into existence

who sacrificed himself
to infuse blood into my veins

whose wings were stripped
& body mulched
for my first bite

yet my first breath was this poison

that pollutes humanity

—

look at all the pigeon feathers
like a garden full of weeds

people let them lie there
like poison ivy

they tremble in the dirt

beautiful & pointless

your affair with god

part one: the finale

i perceived your body
as if it were my wailing wall
& stuck prayers inside your ears.
i rubbed my fingers along the bare surface—
your brittle stone flaked & fell.
you collected in petty piles
each day to be swept.
soon the edges of your existence
were smoothed away & granted,
time had taken the rest.

*

there is an oval of pit
inside my chest. the ruggedness
wears down my meat & muscle,
chafes my bones. the weight
lacerates my skin. the clot,
the it, falls like an asteroid
earthbound & dangerous.

part two: hope

there is an attraction
in the framework
of your body
& now

i piece it together
like a puzzle, my puzzle
that i make whole again
from memory
& you become my naked
artifact. i slide
my fingers down, across,
up, around. you shudder.
there is a breath but it is my breath
& it is trembling.
it reaches for the lips like a rope & grapnel
securing itself, then pulling me.
it draws me to your face & i kiss you.
i kiss you because you are mine
& you are the east light & lamb & unedited
& your passion is the highest proof.
i kiss you because you have texture;
nothing can make you inaccessible.

part three: memories

you drew my hair
behind my ear: "i never
want to let go," & though
you had to, your warmth
has never left.

i'm lost somewhere just below
your nape slowly rising;
i read your body, relax,
listen to the story:
we were made from the same mold,
same material; my mouth created to fit
your mouth—linked, appropriate.

with lives we weren't able to hold,
we spun out of control.
now our arms are each other's stance.

that night we laid in bed
together as a whole:
i mapped out your skin.
you held me like we were lying in snow.
my hand slept, like a lap dog,
on top of yours. i pretended sleep,
not being able to remove myself
from this happiness.
you've become my second skin.
you've become my heart's ornament.

i catch (a hooked fish &
we start to waltz) your eye
at a half glimpse.
(he tightens the line & then)
you turn, slightly, your head
back toward the door (the loosening,
his choice, his longing for the world).
that smile, crests, & like the first touch
into water, it sends shivers; goosebumps
rush over my skin. (i carry you
from the water, my trophy, my
godsend.) i taste you
again & again.

i delight in the mercy of your body,
how it transfers under my fingers
when i massage your skin,
the way it fluctuates

when we make love, the tender
gentleness. how you've come to understand
the anatomy & what pleasures
transpire with touch. you part my lips with your thumb.
you pull down the jaw, to its entirety,
& release your tongue, the tip dances, caresses
the roof of my mouth. i taste
the warm wetness.
i inhale the moment you break open my flesh
& when you're fully between my thighs, i kiss back.

the way that he turned me into
a handful; my body became
burning styrofoam turned to liquid.

—

he lay his head on the pillow of my thigh
curiously
studying the way my cock behaved
in the process of masturbation.

from behind, you gingerly
positioned your fingers amidst my hair
& pulled my head sideways
& pressed your lips to my neck.
you released me & as prompt as my exhale
you left the room
& a knowing basked on the corner of my curved lip.

supine
& exposed

your hands held each cheek
open, waiting, prepared.

i fluently slipped my forefinger
inside, to quench your lust. i am kind,
gentle; i love you. i lower my face

tongue the skin

suck;

you love me. i curl my fingers,
you quiver. your nails dig in my scalp.
you grasp me like i'm about to get away.

you purl, almost like pain.

little earthquake lips

little breaths

are coerced

between your lips

your lips quiver

like   little earthquakes

through your lips

little earthquakes

are coerced

memoir

in the beginning
her eyes
    were mist.

over the years
they turned
    to deep water.

    she'd drown you
in her stare.

a goodbye gun

it is trifling.
i am a revolver
without a bullet.
my chamber spins
wildly. the hammer
clanks hollow blows.
i cannot say hello. i
must go.

the thread that has sewn
two earths together

the spiders
at the corner of the edge
of her world—
slightly above my windowsill.

contently sitting in her web
she studies two distinct planets:
the natural & mine created.
she is the equator.

what they thought was good

mawkish:
a gulag
kept cleansed the land
of rodents

travail, travail
they shall not stop
until death
& death came luscious

camp

his rakish body
helplessly lingered
his soles cracked open

life had a soporific effect
& he was ready
to denounce it to god
stolen: it no longer belonged to him
& he didn't want it anymore

sleeping with buddha

in a dark room
my sight focuses like cat eyes.
my hands mimic the haze around the moon.
something fleeing bumps my neck.

the window is a moth
flown open & the air bites
at its wings. i sit like buddha:
patient & waiting for day to break.

to be the blade

to dance with the blade
to kiss the blade
to take the blade home
to use the blade
to give yourself over to the blade
to feel the blade's coolness
to have the blade inside you
to let the blade tamper with your life

the pregnancy of flies

the yellow-bellied dead
have soaked up the sun.
their stomachs are pregnant
with maggots & dressed
in flies: their wings
glint in the beams: hundreds
of tiny mirrors. the corpses,
heavenly creatures rotting.

About the Author

john compton (b. 1987) is a gay poet who lives in kentucky with his husband josh and their dogs and cats. his latest full length book is "my husband holds my hand because i may drift away & be lost forever in the vortex of a crowded store" published with Flowersong Press (dec 2024); his latest chapbook is "melancholy arcadia" published with Harbor Editions (april 2024).

FLOWERSONG
PRESS

FlowerSong Press nurtures essential verse from, about, and throughout the borderlands. Literary. Lyrical. Boundless.

Sign up for announcements about
new and upcoming titles at:

www.flowersongpress.com

www.ingramcontent.com/pod-product-compliance
Lightning Source LLC
Chambersburg PA
CBHW020424130626
46549CB00006B/2729